Go Fly a Kite, Ben Franklin!

by Peter and Connie Roop

SCHOLASTIC INC.

New York   Toronto   London   Auckland   Sydney
Mexico City   New Delhi   Hong Kong   Buenos Aires

For Ian — always stay as curious as
Ben Franklin!

ISBN 0-439-55442-X

Text copyright © 2003 by Peter and Connie Roop.
Illustrations copyright © 2003 by Scholastic Inc.
All rights reserved. Published by Scholastic Inc.
SCHOLASTIC, BEFORE I MADE HISTORY,
and associated logos are trademarks and/or
registered trademarks of Scholastic Inc.

12 11 10 9 8 7 6 5 4 3 2   3 4 5 6 7 8/0

Printed in the U.S.A.   40
First printing, November 2003

Table of Contents

Introduction

Ben Franklin is a very famous American. He was a printer, an inventor, and a community and national leader. Do you know how he made history?

Ben Franklin was born in Boston. Do you know which city claims Ben as its hero?

Ben Franklin made history with a kite-flying experiment. Do you know he used a metal key in this experiment?

Ben Franklin invented many things. Do you know he gave away his inventions?

Ben Franklin went to elementary school, but never to college. Do you know that he still received college degrees?

For much of his life, Ben Franklin was called Dr. Franklin. Do you know why?

Ben Franklin worked hard all his life. Do you know why he retired from business when he was only forty-two years old?

Ben Franklin is American. Do you know he lived for more than twenty years overseas?

Ben Franklin loved to read. Do you know he created the first joinable library?

Ben Franklin loved to swim. Do you know what he invented to help him swim faster?

Ben Franklin enjoyed writing letters. Do you know what job he had that helped him mail letters?

Ben Franklin signed the Declaration of Independence. Do you know what three other documents he signed that created the United States?

Answers to these questions and many more lie in who Ben Franklin was before he made history!

1
Ben Franklin Is Born

Sunday, January 17, 1706, was cold and sunny in Boston, Massachusetts Colony. The Blue Ball sign at 17 Milk Street swung in the chilly breeze. Downstairs, Josiah Franklin poured hot wax to make candles. Upstairs, Abiah Franklin held her newborn son.

The baby was the fifteenth Franklin child. Josiah and Abiah named him Benjamin after Josiah's favorite brother, Benjamin Franklin. Baby Ben Franklin would grow up to make history.

Baby Ben Franklin had fourteen brothers and sisters. They were Elizabeth, Samuel, Hannah, Josiah, Anne, John, Peter, Mary, James, Sarah, Ebenezer, Thomas, Lydia, and Jane. Josiah and Abiah had two more children after Ben. Two of Ben's brothers had died before he was born.

The Franklin house was crowded and noisy. Ben watched his busy family. Something was always happening. There was always somebody cooking, cleaning, washing, or ironing. Someone was always reading, playing games, making candles or soap, or spinning wool. Someone was always talking or singing.

At night, friends stopped by to talk with Josiah Franklin. Josiah was poor, but he was respected. People listened to what he had to say about religion, family, and politics. If someone was in trouble, Josiah gladly gave advice. Josiah invited special people to share Franklin meals. He wanted his children to hear good conversations and to be curious about their world. Ben remembered being so interested in the conversations that he forgot what he had eaten. After dinner, Josiah played his violin and sang hymns.

Ben explored his busy world. He was curious, especially about books. He watched

his family reading and wanted to learn this skill. Ben taught himself how to read. By age five, Ben was reading the Bible, sermons, newspapers, and every book he could get his hands on. Later, Ben wrote, "I do not remember when I could not read." All his life, Ben Franklin loved words. He read them, wrote them, printed them, and spoke them.

In 1712, when he was six years old, Ben's family moved to a bigger house. Mr. Franklin hung his Blue Ball sign over his new shop and home. Here he made candles and soap and raised his large family. Ben Franklin lived here for six years.

The Franklins lived near the center of Boston. Their home was close to the docks where ships arrived from all around the world. Ben liked to stare at the tall ships. He dreamed of one day becoming a sailor.

When Ben was young, Boston was the biggest, busiest town in America. There were things to see and do all around the town. Carpenters built buildings. Blacksmiths hammered metal at their glowing forges. Farmers rolled into town with wagons loaded with fruits, vegetables, and meat. Pigs rooted for food. Sailors strolled down the cobblestone streets. Bricklayers laid rows of red bricks for more homes, shops, and markets. Shopkeepers greeted customers. Children ran errands and played games. Boston fascinated Ben. He learned a lot from wandering the streets. Soon, he learned even more.

In 1713, when he was seven years old, Ben's love of reading turned into a lifelong love of writing. Ben taught himself how to write, and he wrote poems. He begged his father to send his poems to his uncle Benjamin Franklin in England. Uncle Benjamin told Ben how much he enjoyed the poems. Ben was thrilled! He learned about the pleasures of writing.

That same year, Ben learned an important lesson about money. Ben was given some coins to spend on anything he liked. He dashed to the toy store. Along the way, he met a boy blowing a whistle. Ben enjoyed the loud music the boy played. Ben wanted his own whistle.

Ben gave the boy all his coins and ran home, proudly tooting his new whistle. The noisy whistle annoyed Ben's family, but he was pleased. That is, until Ben told his family how much he had paid for the whistle. They laughed at him, saying they could have bought four whistles for what Ben paid for one! Ben cried, thinking about the other toys he could have bought.

Making wise purchases was a lesson Ben never forgot. When he saw people wasting money, Ben reminded himself, "Poor man, you pay too much for your whistle."

2
Ben Learns More Lessons

Ben was fun to play with. He had many friends, and Ben was their leader. The boys went fishing, swimming, boating, and canoeing. Ben admitted that sometimes he led his friends into "scrapes."

One scrape taught Ben a lesson about honesty. Ben and his friends were trying to catch minnows in a pond. They trampled the mud so much that the water turned brown. They could not see the fish. Ben noticed a pile of stones being used to build a house, and he had an idea. *Why not build our own dock with the stones?* Ben thought.

That evening, Ben and his friends worked like ants, building their rock dock. The next morning, the workers found all their stones

missing. They saw Ben's dock and realized that Ben and his friends had taken their rocks. The boys had to return all the heavy rocks. Ben explained to his father that their work had been useful. Mr. Franklin explained to Ben that he had stolen someone's property. Ben said his father "convinced me that nothing was useful which was not honest."

Ben learned another lesson at the pond. When he was curious about something, he tried to understand it. He wanted to learn how to swim. In those days, few people knew how to swim. There was no one to teach Ben, so he taught himself.

While swimming, Ben learned another lesson. Sometimes Ben swam so much he grew tired. He decided to solve his problem. He watched ducks swim with their webbed feet. If ducks could swim so well, Ben Franklin could, too! Ben made paddles and attached them to his hands and feet. The paddles were hard to use. Ben had the right idea, but it didn't work as well as he expected. So he tried another idea.

Ben enjoyed flying kites. Sometimes they pulled him forward. *Would my kite pull me through the water?* Ben wondered. He would find out!

Ben waded into the pond. The wind pulled his kite high into the sky. Holding the string tightly, Ben floated on the water. Slowly, the kite pulled Ben across the pond. His kite experiment had worked!

Ben learned another lifelong lesson. If at first you don't succeed, try, try again.

But not all of Ben's lessons came from his outdoor experiences. In 1714, when Ben was eight years old, his father said it was time for Ben to go to school. In those days, few children went to school. Most boys learned a trade from their fathers. Most girls learned how to take good care of a house so one day they could manage their own homes.

Josiah Franklin knew that Ben was very intelligent. He planned for Ben to be a minister when he grew up, so Ben had to go to school, including college. Ben went to Boston Latin School. Soon, Ben was at the top of his class. He did so well that he skipped the next grade!

Ben didn't have the chance to skip a grade. Josiah didn't have enough money to send Ben to Boston Latin School. Ben went to George Brownwell's school, which he liked. Mr. Brownwell taught writing and math. Ben's writing skills improved, especially his handwriting. But Ben struggled with math.

Josiah changed his mind. Ben wouldn't become a minister. Ben would become a candle maker, like Josiah.

In 1716, Ben worked in his father's shop. He snipped candlewicks and poured steamy wax into candle molds. He melted fat in hot pots and made soap. He ran errands and sold things. Ten-year-old Ben and sixty-year-old Josiah worked sixteen long hours every day except Sunday.

Ben hated almost every boring minute of it. He needed something else to keep his curious mind busy.

3
Ben Becomes an Apprentice

Ben turned to books. Ben decided that if he couldn't go to school, he would teach himself. Ben read every chance he could. One of his favorite books was *The Pilgrim's Progress* by John Bunyan. Ben liked the book so much that whenever he had a little money, he wisely spent it on a set of Bunyan's books.

Ben read about famous Greeks and Romans. He read about earthquakes, famous women, and Robinson Crusoe. He bought fifty small, inexpensive history books.

After two years, Ben was tired of the candle and soap business. He told his father that he wanted to be a sailor. Josiah saw how unhappy his son was, but he said that Ben could not be a sailor. He agreed that Ben could quit the candle business if he learned another trade. A boy had to have a trade to earn a living when he was older.

Ben couldn't decide what trade he wanted to learn. In 1718, when Ben was twelve years old, Josiah took him on long walks around Boston to look at different trades. That way, Ben could pick which trade he would learn.

Ben watched carpenters hammering and bricklayers spreading mortar. He saw rope makers twisting rope and sail makers stitching sails. He observed cobblers making shoes and blacksmiths shaping horseshoes. He watched coopers building barrels and millers grinding grain. He saw shipwrights constructing ships and silversmiths polishing silver.

Ben enjoyed watching the tradesmen working. Ben said, "It has ever since been a pleasure for me to see good workmen handle their tools." Ben learned enough from his observations to be able to do jobs around his own home when he grew older. Ben also learned how to make "little machines for my experiments," a skill he used to become a fa-

mous scientist. But Ben didn't see any trade he wanted to learn.

So Josiah made up Ben's mind for him (something Ben did not like!). Ben would become a cutler and make knives. Ben went to work for his cousin Samuel Franklin.

Ben was home three days later when Samuel asked for money to teach Ben. Josiah said he wouldn't pay, especially since Samuel's father was living in the overcrowded Franklin house for free!

Suddenly, Josiah realized what trade was just right for Ben. Ben loved to read and write. Ben could be a printer! And who better to teach him than James, Ben's big brother!

In 1718, when he was twelve years old, Ben signed an agreement with James. Ben would work for James until 1727, when Ben was twenty-one years old. Ben would not be paid until the last year. James agreed to feed Ben, give him a home, provide him with clothes, and teach him the printer's trade. Ben beamed. He was a printer's apprentice!

At first, Ben didn't like being a printer's

apprentice. James gave Ben the worst jobs. Ben had to be up before dawn to carry in wood and build fires. He pumped water for drinking and cleaning. He ran errands and swept the floor. He waited on customers. Ben did everything but print!

Ben was eager to learn how to print a pamphlet, almanac, sermon, or book. He watched James set lead letters in wooden trays to make words. He saw him roll black ink onto the letters and carefully place a sheet of paper onto the inked letters. Ben watched James pull the heavy handle, pressing the paper onto the letters.

Finally, James taught Ben these skills. Ben learned quickly. Soon he was setting the type to spell words, inking the paper, and handling the press like an expert. The work was hard, but Ben didn't mind. He was strong from swimming and easily lifted the heavy boxes of letters. The days were long. James and Ben worked fifteen hours a day. Ben didn't mind. He had worked longer hours for his father.

All his life, Ben was involved with printing. When he was seventy-five years old and living in France, Ben had a printing press. Ben had a lifelong love of words.

Ben kept reading, too. He woke up early to read before the shop became busy. He read by candlelight late at night when the shop was empty. He read on Sundays when everyone was at church.

Books were expensive, however, and Ben had little money. He borrowed books from friends and family. Still, he couldn't get enough books.

One of Ben's friends was a bookseller's apprentice. Ben begged his friend to lend him a book after the bookseller's shop closed each evening. Ben stayed up late and got up even earlier to finish reading the book. Ben returned the book to his friend before the bookshop opened in the morning.

Matthew Adams, a frequent customer at the printing shop, saw how much Ben enjoyed reading. He kindly let Ben borrow books from his own collection. Ben read essays, science and history books, and novels.

4
Ben Becomes a Writer — and a Runaway!

Ben kept writing. He wrote a poem called "The Lighthouse Tragedy" and another about Blackbeard, the pirate. James liked Ben's poems so much that he printed them. Ben sold his poems around Boston. This came to an end when Ben's father read the poems. He told Ben that his poems were terrible and that poets were no better than beggars.

Ben stopped writing poems. Later he said, "So I escaped being a poet, most probably a very bad one."

Ben tried to improve himself. He mastered math. He wrote a list of things to do to become a better person: be a better listener, save money, be clean, work hard, and be nice to others.

Ben always needed money to buy more books. Ben had an idea! James paid for his apprentices to eat out. Ben convinced James to give him half of what James paid for Ben's meals. James thought this was a good idea. He would save money. Ben thought it was a great bargain, too. He spent the money for bread, fruit, and vegetables. He drank water. Ben spent his extra money on books. Ben said, "Eat to live, and not live to eat."

In 1721, when Ben was fifteen years old, James began printing the *New England Courant* newspaper. People enjoyed reading the news. Humorous stories were another favorite part of the paper.

Ben had an idea! He would write funny stories for the newspaper. Ben knew James would not publish the stories if he realized Ben had written them. So Ben created the character of Silence Dogood to tell his stories. Silence Dogood was a widow who made funny observations about the world.

Ben changed his handwriting so James wouldn't recognize it. One night, Ben slipped his first Silence Dogood story under the printing house door. James was delighted with Silence Dogood's story and published it in his newspaper. The readers of the *New England Courant* were delighted with Silence Dogood, too. They eagerly bought more newspapers. James was happy!

The fourteen Silence Dogood stories were so successful that Ben wanted James to know he had written them. Ben told James that he was Silence Dogood. Instead of being pleased with Ben's cleverness, James was angry that Ben had tricked him.

James was now mean to Ben. He gave him extra work. He hit him. Even though he was still his brother's apprentice, Ben decided to run away. Ben felt it was better to break his agreement with his unpleasant brother than suffer in his shop any longer.

Ben Franklin was seventeen years old. *Where will I go? What will I do for money?* Ben worried.

Books were the only things Ben owned that had any value. He had no choice. Ben sold his precious books to buy a ticket for a ship sailing to New York. Ben chose New York because it was the nearest large city with printing shops. He hoped to get work as a printer.

In New York, Ben went to William Bradford's printing shop. Mr. Bradford didn't have a job for Ben. He suggested that Ben ask his son Andrew if he needed help in his printing shop in Philadelphia.

Philadelphia was one hundred miles away. Ben sent his trunk with his extra clothes by ship. He traveled overland. On the way, Ben had many adventures. He was in a terrible storm. He saved a man's life. He got very sick. He walked fifty miles. He rowed a boat all night.

Finally, on a Sunday morning in 1723, a dirty, tired Ben Franklin set foot in Philadelphia for the first time. Neither Ben nor Philadelphia would ever be the same.

Ben knew no one. He did not know where

he would live. His spare shirt and stockings were stuffed into his pockets. He was starving. And he had only one dollar!

Ben found a bakery on Market Street and bought three large loaves of bread. Ben was surprised at the amount of bread he could buy for three pennies. Ben stuck a loaf under each arm and walked up Market Street, chewing on the third loaf. Suddenly, he heard a girl laughing at him! Ben smiled, knowing he looked a little ridiculous.

Later, Ben found out the girl's name was Deborah Read. One day, Deborah and Ben would marry.

5
Ben in Philadelphia

Ben walked on, eating his bread. When he had eaten one loaf he was full. Ben generously gave the other two loaves to a hungry mother and daughter.

Ben saw some nicely dressed Quakers on their way to their meetinghouse for a worship service. Ben followed them into the meetinghouse, sat down, and fell fast asleep. When the service ended, Ben woke up and left.

Ben met a boy who took him to an inexpensive lodging house. He spent the last of his money paying for a bed. Ben went to sleep early, because he knew he must find work the next day.

In the morning, Ben went to Andrew

Bradford's shop. Unfortunately, Andrew had no work for Ben. He suggested that Ben go to Samuel Keimer's printing shop.

Mr. Keimer was new to the printing business. His printing press was old. Mr. Keimer desperately needed help, and he hired Ben. Ben Franklin had his first paying job.

Mr. Keimer sent Ben next door to see if the family living there had a room that Ben could rent. Imagine Ben's surprise when Deborah Read, the girl who had laughed at him, opened the door! Her family had a room, and Ben moved in.

Ben worked hard for Mr. Keimer. He fixed his printing press and cleaned the shop. He set the letters and did the printing. Mr. Keimer liked Ben, especially since Ben did all the work! Ben came to work early, worked hard all day, read, and went to sleep early.

One day, a very successful Ben Franklin would write, "Early to bed, early to rise, makes a man healthy, wealthy, and wise." In 1723, Ben was already practicing these habits.

Ben easily made friends in Philadelphia.

But he kept the fact that he had run away from Boston a secret.

As usual, Ben pinched every penny to buy books. He borrowed books from his new friends. He walked the streets of Philadelphia, enjoying the hustle and bustle of the growing city. Ben forgot about his miserable life with James in Boston.

One day, Ben had a shock. His secret was out! His brother-in-law, Captain Robert Holmes, had learned Ben was in Philadelphia. He wrote Ben a letter, saying that his parents and brother forgave him.

Ben wrote back, explaining why he left Boston and saying his family did not need to forgive him, because he had done nothing wrong. Captain Holmes enjoyed Ben's letter so much he showed it to Sir William Keith, the governor of Pennsylvania.

Sir William was very impressed with the quality of Ben's writing. He wanted to meet this outstanding young man who used words so well. Mr. Keimer beamed when Sir William entered his shop. He had never had such an important visitor. But Sir William had not come to see Mr. Keimer. He had come to see Benjamin Franklin! Ben said that Mr. Keimer "stared like a pig poisoned."

Sir William told Ben that if he would set up his own printing shop, Sir William would give him Pennsylvania's and Delaware's government printing work. Sir William suggested that Ben return to Boston and borrow money from his father.

So in April 1724, Ben sailed to Boston. He was eighteen years old. The Franklins were pleased to have Ben home. That is, everyone except James. When Ben went to his brother's printing shop, James was not happy to see how successful Ben had become. Ben wore a suit and had money. The apprentices asked Ben questions about his new life. Ben answered them, showed them his watch (a rare thing for a young man to own), and gave them money so they could buy a treat.

This made James very angry. He said Ben "had insulted him in such a manner before his people that he could never forget or forgive it."

Ben asked his father if he could borrow money to open his own shop in Philadelphia. Josiah told Ben he was too young. He should work hard and save his own money.

Ben returned to Philadelphia, where he had a surprise. Sir William would lend Ben the money!

Ben needed a printing press, lead letters, and other tools to open his shop. These supplies could only be bought in London. Ben would have to travel to England.

Sir William promised to give Ben the money for his supplies. Ben would receive the money when he reached London. Ben was excited! He would work hard and be a success.

Ben felt so good that he asked Deborah Read to marry him. Deborah agreed, but Mrs. Read said they would have to wait until Ben returned from London.

On November 5, 1724, eighteen-year-old Benjamin Franklin sailed for England. Ben had no idea he would later cross the wide Atlantic Ocean seven more times.

6

Ben in London

When Ben arrived in London, he set foot in the world's largest city. But Ben was in for a disappointing surprise. Sir William Keith's money wasn't there! Ben learned that Sir William often made promises he didn't keep.

Ben was far from home, with little money and no friends. Rather than feel sorry for himself, Ben found work at Palmer's print shop. He then moved to Watt's shop, where forty printers worked. Ben quickly impressed his printing companions. To save money, he drank only water. To get exercise, he carried two trays of heavy lead letters while the others carried one. Ben ate vegetables, which were cheap and healthy.

Ben also impressed the shop owner, who liked the fact that Ben worked long hours without complaining. He was pleased that Ben came to work every Monday on time and that he did his work quickly. Soon he gave Ben better printing jobs and more pay.

Ben tried to save his hard-earned money, but there were so many ways to spend it in London! Ben went to the theater and to concerts. He bought books. He went boating. Much to the amazement of his friends, Ben swam in the Thames River. He even gave swimming lessons!

Ben spent so much money that he had none left over to return to America. After eighteen months, however, Ben grew homesick. He wanted to marry Deborah Read and own a business. He enjoyed his life in London, but he now wanted to return to Philadelphia.

Ben met Thomas Denham, a merchant from Philadelphia. Mr. Denham was returning to America to open a store. He needed an honest, hardworking clerk and offered Ben the job. Ben accepted, thinking he would never be a printer again.

On July 23, 1726, Ben and Mr. Denham set sail for Philadelphia. Ben was twenty years old.

Ben liked his time at sea. He read. He talked with his fellow passengers. He enjoyed watching dolphins swim around the ship. He collected seaweed and crabs. He wrote about flying fish. He observed the wind and weather. When the wind didn't blow and the ship didn't move, Ben swam in the ocean. Always curious, Ben even studied the sharks swimming near him!

But Ben was ready to work for Mr. Denham when the ship docked in Philadelphia on October 11, 1726. Ben was home, and this time he meant to stay!

Life, however, did not work out the way Ben had planned. Deborah had grown tired of waiting for Ben and had married John Rogers. After opening the store, Ben and Mr.

Denham got sick. Ben recovered, but Mr. Denham died. Ben was on his own again. He turned to what he knew best: printing.

Ben went to Mr. Keimer, who was glad to see him. He immediately gave Ben a job with good pay. Mr. Keimer needed Ben. Business was poor. The shop was a mess. The workers knew little about printing.

Before long, Ben trained the workers to do their jobs better. As usual, Ben set a good example by coming to work early and staying late. He made the customers happy.

Once the shop was running smoothly, Mr. Keimer lowered Ben's wages. Ben quit, and so did Ben's friend, Hugh Meredith. Hugh's father had money that he wanted to invest in a business. Mr. Meredith admired Ben's skills and his willingness to work hard. He loaned the money to Ben and Hugh so that they could open a printing shop.

Ben worked even harder now. He dressed his best to impress customers. He brought printing paper down the street in a wheelbarrow so people could see how hard he worked. He paid his bills on time. He didn't hunt or fish. He saved his money. Ben followed his own advice: "A penny saved is a penny earned."

To make more money, Ben decided to start a newspaper. But before he could, Mr. Keimer began publishing the *Pennsylvania Gazette*. Ben began writing for the *Mercury*, a rival newspaper. With Ben's help, the *Mercury* sold well. The *Pennsylvania Gazette* did not. After nine months, Mr. Keimer sold his newspaper to Ben and Hugh. Hugh, however, had grown tired of the printing business, so he sold his share of the shop to Ben.

7
Ben in Business

By 1729, when he was twenty-three years old, Ben Franklin finally owned a printing business! He had a press and a newspaper. Ben also sold pens, paper, ink, maps, tea, coffee, groceries, books, and soap made by his father. Ben was the first bookseller outside of Boston. Ben advertised his goods in his newspaper, and more people came to his shop.

Ben had more good news. Deborah's husband had left her, and now she could marry Ben. On September 1, 1730, Deborah became Ben's wife. Ben had made a good choice. Deborah was as hardworking as Ben and as determined as Ben to be successful. Soon she was helping in the shop. She sewed pam-

phlet pages together. She served customers. She cooked simple, inexpensive meals.

Ben and Deborah had three children: William, Francis, and Sally. Unfortunately, Francis died of smallpox when he was four years old. Thirty-six years after Francis died, Ben said, "To this day I cannot think of [Francis] without a sigh."

Ben and Deborah worked very hard. Within two years of their marriage, they did not owe a single penny to anyone.

Ben Franklin was known around Philadelphia as a hardworking, pleasant young man with a fine future. Ben enjoyed the printing business. He met people, talked with them, and found out their thoughts.

Ben invited eleven eager young men like himself to get together on Friday evenings to share ideas. The men asked questions, solved business problems, and thought about how they could improve their lives. Ben called his club the Junto.

Ben wanted more books, as usual. He had an idea! *What if all the members of the Junto shared their books with one another?* Ben wondered. The Junto members agreed, and Ben had more books to read.

A year later, Ben improved his idea. He started a library for everyone in Philadelphia. To join, you had to pay money, which was used to buy books. This was called a subscription library. Fifty people joined, and a book order was sent to London.

In October 1731, when Ben was twenty-five years old, the library opened. People in other towns learned of Ben's library and began their own. Ben's was the first subscription library in America, but soon there were dozens.

Ben knew not everyone could afford to join his library, so he had another idea. He would publish a small, cheap book called an almanac. Ben's almanac would be packed with information, calendars, weather predictions, jokes, words of wisdom, and funny thoughts.

Ben decided to write the almanac under a different name. In Boston, he had been known as Silence Dogood. In Philadelphia, he would be Poor Richard. In December 1732, when Ben was twenty-six years old, *Poor Richard's Almanack* was published for the first time.

Poor Richard was an immediate hit. People laughed at his jokes. They chuckled at his problems with his proud wife. They thought about his wise sayings like "Haste makes waste" and "The cat in gloves catches no mice."

Ben's almanac became popular throughout the thirteen American colonies. His words were enjoyed as far away as France, where Poor Richard was known as Bonhomme Richard.

Ben published his almanac until 1758. It was a best-seller everywhere. Only the Bible sold more copies! Poor Richard made Ben Franklin a rich man.

8

Ben Flies a Kite
and Changes the World

Ben's thoughts turned to improving life in
Philadelphia. Ben always believed in doing
good for others. Through his newspaper and
friends, Ben worked to make Philadelphia a
safer, cleaner, nicer place to live. Ben didn't
like the dusty, dirty streets of Philadelphia,
so he worked to get them paved with cobble-
stones. At night, it was too dark to safely go
around town, so Ben worked to get street-
lights.

Fire was a great danger in Philadelphia
because so many buildings were made out of
wood. In 1736, Ben organized Philadelphia's

first fire department. Soon, other fire groups were organized.

Ben organized watchmen to protect people and homes at night. He worked to create the first hospital in America. He remembered how expensive it had been to go to school when he was a boy, so Ben began a free school. He also began a college. Today, this college is the University of Pennsylvania. Philadelphia was a much nicer town now, thanks to Ben.

Ben also had ideas on how to improve life at home. Fireplaces smoked too much, burned too much wood, and did not give off much heat. Ben invented a stove that burned less wood, sent hot air into a room to make it warmer, and sent the smoke up the chimney. The stove was called the Franklin stove. Ben gave his idea away so everyone's lives would be better.

Ben did so well with his printing business that he decided to retire. In 1748, when he was forty-two years old, Ben sold his business. He wanted to use his time to make the world a better place and to "read, study, and make experiments." As Ben wrote in *Poor Richard's Almanack*, "Lost time is never found again."

Ben had always been curious. He became very interested in electricity. At this time, electrical sparks were played with for entertainment. Tricks were performed. Sparks were pulled out of people's ears. Ben even tried to cook a turkey with electricity from a battery. The electrical shock was so strong that it knocked Ben out before he could cook his turkey!

Ben thought there was more to electricity than just games. He wondered if lightning and electricity were the same. Lightning was a major problem for people because it hit their wooden homes and burned them down.

Ben had an idea! He thought that if a person put a metal rod on his house, lightning would hit the rod and travel into the ground. The house would not burn down. Ben didn't try his rod idea, but he told other scientists about it.

Ben remembered his boyhood days when he flew kites. What if he flew a kite during a thunderstorm? Lightning would hit the kite and travel down the string, where he could feel it. *Was lightning really electricity?* Ben wondered.

In September 1752, Ben and his son, William, flew a kite during a thunderstorm. The kite danced at one end of a long string. A key dangled at the end Ben held. Lightning crashed! Thunder boomed!

Suddenly, Ben saw loose threads on the string standing up, a sign of electricity. Ben held his knuckle out to the key. A brilliant spark leaped from the key to Ben's hand. Electricity!

Ben had proven that lightning was electricity. And he was incredibly lucky, because he could have easily been killed by the lightning.

Ben decided to test his idea about lightning rods attached to houses. Ben didn't know this, but six months before, a French scientist had already tried Ben's lightning rod idea, and it had worked!

Ben attached a lightning rod to his own home. Soon other people did the same thing. Today, lightning rods are used on buildings worldwide to protect them from lightning. As usual, Ben gave his valuable idea away!

Ben's fame as the tamer of lightning spread throughout the colonies. Harvard College and Yale College honored Ben with degrees. People in Europe were fascinated with Ben's discovery. In November 1753, when he was forty-seven years old, Ben was given the Copley Medal, the highest scientific award in the world.

Ben Franklin had made history! But there was still much more history for him to make.

9
Ben Becomes Famous

In 1753, Ben was named Postmaster General of the thirteen American colonies. It was his job to make sure that the mail reached each colony. But the roads were rough, and no one was sure how far it was between cities. Ben invented the odometer, which he attached to his carriage wheel. As the wheel turned, the odometer measured how far the carriage had traveled. Ben visited each colony. With his new odometer, he now knew exactly how far it was between cities.

Ben was one of the few people who had ever visited each of the thirteen colonies. He met people and heard their complaints. Ben Franklin knew America and Americans better than anyone else.

Ben was very popular in Pennsylvania. People knew he could solve difficult problems, so they elected him to the Pennsylvania Assembly. There, Ben could help run the colony.

But the most important decisions about the Pennsylvania Colony were being made in London. Ben was asked to go to England to help solve a tax problem. In 1757, at age fifty-one, Ben sailed to London again.

Ben was pleased to be back in England where he had spent eighteen enjoyable months when he was younger. Now he was famous. People everywhere wanted to meet the man who had tamed lightning. Ben was invited to parties and dinners. Scientists wanted to discuss his ideas and inventions. In Edinburgh, Scotland, Ben was given a Doctor of Laws degree by Edinburgh University. Now he was Dr. Benjamin Franklin!

Even with all of the attention, Ben did not forget his work on getting the tax laws changed. But it took him five years!

In 1762, Ben returned home to Philadelphia. Ben planned to rest, read, think, invent, and be with his family. Events in America and England would soon change Ben's plans.

Other colonies were upset about the taxes the English placed on them. The English believed they could control the American colonies. England was three thousand miles away. Americans felt that decisions involving them should be made in America, especially decisions about taxes. In 1764, Ben returned to England to help solve these problems and others, too.

That year, the English passed the Stamp Act. This meant that Americans had to pay a tax on all the sugar, paper, tea, coffee, and newspapers they bought from England. And they weren't allowed to buy from any other countries!

Many Americans were angry about this stamp tax. They said it was unfair that Americans had no representatives in the English Parliament, where the tax laws were made.

Ben was upset, too, so he used his wit, charm, intelligence, and energy to change the law. And he did! In 1766, the stamp law ended.

Ben was a hero in America. People were proud of his inventions and his work as a diplomat. Ben now had time to travel around England and Europe. He met King Louis XV of France. He went to parties and dinners. He did experiments. He began writing a book about his fascinating life.

But trouble returned in 1767, when England passed new tax laws. King George III believed that he had the right to make the Americans pay taxes to England. The Americans disagreed. They stopped buying tea, coffee, paper, glass, and other things from England.

Ben worked to get these unfair taxes changed. In 1770, Ben's efforts paid off. All the new taxes except one were dropped. Only tea would still be taxed. King George III wanted the Americans to know he had the power to do what he wanted to the colonies.

Ben thought that if England and America could not be friends, they would become enemies. The thirteen American colonies might even want their independence from England!

In 1773, an event happened that split Americans further from the English. An English ship loaded with tea entered Boston harbor. The English said the tea tax had to be paid. The Americans said they would never pay it!

One dark night in December 1773, American patriots disguised as Native Americans slipped onboard the ship. They dumped the hated tea into the sea. Americans celebrated this Boston Tea Party. The English were angry. King George III sent an army to live in Boston until the tea was paid for.

On April 19, 1775, English soldiers shot at American patriots at Lexington and Concord, Massachusetts. American patriots shot back. The Revolutionary War had begun! George Washington was made general of the American army.

Ben knew it was time for him to leave England. His English friends were now his enemies.

10
Ben Helps Create
the United States

Ben arrived home on May 5, 1775. He was sixty-nine years old. He was sick. His legs hurt so much he could hardly walk. His wife, Deborah, had died while he was gone. Ben longed for peace and quiet.

Instead, he was pushed into the Revolution. America needed Ben's help, and he was glad to give it.

Representatives from the thirteen colonies were meeting in Philadelphia. Ben was elected to go to this Continental Congress. The Congress decided that the thirteen colonies should declare their independence from

England. The colonies would become the United States of America.

On June 24, 1776, Ben was asked to serve on a committee to write the Declaration of Independence. Thomas Jefferson did most of the writing. Ben shared his expertise as a writer and made minor changes.

On July 4, 1776, the Declaration of Independence was adopted. Knowing the seriousness of their decision to form a new nation, Ben said, "We must all hang together, or assuredly we shall all hang separately."

Ben was seventy years old, too old to carry a gun in the war for independence. But his help was still needed.

The United States had to have friends to help defeat England. France had long been an enemy of England. France might help. Who better to ask France for help than the famous Dr. Benjamin Franklin?

Ben was in France by the end of 1776. He was wildly popular. He wore a coonskin cap. He went to parties and special dinners. Ben's image was on plates, boxes, and rings. Ben

said his face was "as well known as that of the moon."

At first, France would not help the United States. The Americans had lost too many battles. Then, in 1777, the Americans captured five thousand English soldiers. The French king thought the Americans might just win against his hated English enemies. He said France would help the United States. They would give money, guns, supplies, and ships.

One ship the French gave was the *Bonhomme Richard*, named in honor of Franklin and his almanac. The *Bonhomme Richard* was the first American ship to defeat a huge English ship called a man-of-war.

The Revolutionary War dragged on until 1781, when the Americans defeated the English at Yorktown. England agreed to sign a peace treaty with the United States. Who should sign the treaty for America? None other than Benjamin Franklin!

In 1785, when he was seventy-nine years old, Ben returned to Philadelphia. He wanted to come home quietly. Instead, there was a great celebration. Church bells rang. Cannons fired. Flags fluttered. Thousands of people cheered their hero at his homecoming.

The thirteen independent states now needed a government to make sure there were laws that treated people equally and fairly. Certainly, wise old Ben Franklin would have some advice.

He did. Ben worked on writing the Constitution of the United States. These laws would help govern the young country Ben loved so much. On March 4, 1789, Ben signed the Constitution. On April 30, 1789, George Washington became the first President of the United States.

Ben Franklin was the only American to sign all four documents that created the United States: the Declaration of Independence, the treaty with France, the peace treaty with England, and the Constitution.

But Ben's work was not finished. He argued for the turkey to become the symbol of America instead of the bald eagle. This was one of Ben's ideas that didn't work so well!

Ben asked Congress to end slavery. He wrote letters to faraway friends, sharing ideas and giving advice. American friends frequently stopped by to chat with Ben.

Benjamin Franklin was now eighty-four years old. He had spent his life helping others, and he was worn out. On April 17, 1790, Ben died in his sleep. Ben Franklin had written in *Poor Richard's Almanack*, "If you would not be forgotten, as soon as you are dead and rotten, either write things worth reading, or do things worth the writing."

As usual, Benjamin Franklin had followed his own advice. Who would have guessed all Ben Franklin would accomplish when he was born that cold January day in 1706?